FINISHING

21 TOOLS GUARANTEED TO HELP YOU REACH YOUR GOALS, EVEN WHEN THINGS GET TOUGH

EVAN LACON

BARKING DOG BOOKS

Copyright © 2017 of Evan Lacon

Originally published through Amazon Digital Services LLC

Image on page 22 courtesy of Pixabay.com

Design by Jessica Jenkins

*To the mountain, where I would
go daily for inspiration.*

*To my faithful and beloved dog, Binks,
who was with me every step of the way.*

*To all my teachers, for showing me
that anything is possible.*

*And to me, for wanting to write
a book and Finishing it.*

CONGRATULATIONS FOR BUYING THIS BOOK.

You have just taken a very important first step in accomplishing something that's important to you. I'm assuming you are here because you want something different out of life and you're ready to make that happen. Many people dream about success or achieving a big goal but can't seem to make it happen. They start a project, dream of a new career, desperately want a different body or some other lifelong ambition, only to end up right back where they started. If that's been you in the past, rest assured, things are about to change! This book was written with you in mind. It doesn't matter what goals you want to achieve, be it big or small. Whether you're just beginning something you have always dreamed of or stuck in the middle of an ongoing pursuit that you just can't finish. Whether you're a newbie at self development or have been a lifelong learner of ways to make your life better, this book will give you the ability to learn and practice 21 of the most powerful and effective tools for accomplishing your goals and achieving lasting success in any area of your life.

True and lasting success requires the right state of mind, support, inspiration, and developing effective success habits. This book will introduce you to 21 of the most effective, easy-to-use tools for doing just that. In addition, you will learn how to put each of these tools into action and experience immediate success. As you work with them, your life will change. You will succeed and grow. Your new found self-confidence and intuition will supplement worry and fear.

I say with complete confidence both from my own personal journey and my experience in helping over a thousand people achieve their goals, if you take these tools to heart, your life will change in ways you have only dreamed of and ways not yet imagined. These tools work!

TABLE OF CONTENTS

WHY TOOLS?

"THE RIGHT TOOL FOR THE RIGHT JOB."

—UNKNOWN

All forms of creation require tools. We understand this when we think about erecting buildings, cooking meals, fixing broken machines or managing data. We accept that tools enable us to do what we could never do ourselves. In addition, we pride ourselves on our ability to choose the right tool for a specific job and use it in a way that creates the best results.

For many of us, when it comes to our personal success, this concept of relying on tools is not so obvious. Most people don't think about what set of tools they will need to employ today to help them lose that stubborn fifteen pounds, write that book, or double their incomes from the previous year. We believe that personal success is mysterious and for others who have better luck, more money, or are more qualified. Nothing could be further from the truth. From childhood, we are taught, and come to believe that we should be able to accomplish anything on our own, that hard work and persistence alone will

1

save the day. While this is partially true, it is by no means the whole story. In fact, this belief on your ability to go it alone, can lead to feelings of failure and low self-esteem as we try and fail, try and fail again or simply give up on our dreams.

The truth is, that fulfilling a personal goal is like building that skyscraper. In both case the better able we are to choose and correctly use the right tool the more likely we are to get the job done and succeed. Once we combine the right tool(s) with our own abilities we become unstoppable!

The tools you will learn about here will compliment your own abilities and give you that extra juice you need to reach the finish line. Remember we are wired to continually evolve and learn. To always search out and employ new strategies and tools that make us better along this journey we call life.

As any cook, engineer, or success coach will tell you, choosing the right tool for a job is key to getting it done efficiently and well. For many of us, being shown which tools are best for a job is all we need. Something clicks inside and we run with it, growing and succeeding in new and wonderful ways.

I love to cook. As you can imagine, one of the most important tools I use in the kitchen to make great food are knives. But which knife? Here is the key to understanding tools. Some tools make our jobs easier and others don't. Using cooking as an example, if I'm chopping veggies for a salad, the knife that works best is my eight-inch chef's knife. This knife fits nicely in my hand, has just the right weight and allows me to chop efficiently and safely. In contrast, when I'm eating dinner and cutting chicken, I'll use a steak knife; it's got a nice wooden handle, a serrated blade, and fits perfectly in my hand. It's big enough to cut chicken well, but small enough to rest comfortably on my plate when I'm not cutting. I would never use my steak knife for chopping veggies nor my chef's knife for cutting my dinner. They simply wouldn't work well and would make my job so much harder. So finding and using the correct tool to help you accomplish your personal or professional goals will allow you to succeed and have fun along the way.

Every successful business owner, CEO, or high achiever will tell you that their ability to leverage the effective use of tools was key to their success and the success of their organizations.

By the time, you are done reading this book, you will come to understand and appreciate the enormous part tools play in achieving success of any kind. You will recognize which tools you are now using that are working well and contribute to your current success and which new ones you will need to employ to achieve new goals.

Don't stress out, all the tools you'll learn about here will make your life easier. Imagine if you will, being able to swim downstream instead of upstream. Or cycling with the wind at your back verses on your face. These analogies are perfect for the way you will move thru life once you begin to practice what you will learn here. Let these success tools do all the heavy lifting as you. Let them help you soar toward your goals and reach success.

All the tools you will discover here, will create lasting positive effects long after you have reached your initial goal. As you read this book and practice these tools, you will be developing new ways of looking at the world and learning highly effective strategies for accomplishing anything now and in the future.

UNDERSTANDING AND CREATING YOUR OWN PERSONAL SUCCESS TOOLKIT

If you're like most people you probably have a toolkit, toolbox or junk drawer at home filled with essential tools. Even if you're not handy, you most likely have a few of the basics; a screw driver, hammer, wrench, tape measure and scissors for example. Just as you would grab the tool you need when doing a project around the house, so will you grab tools from this book to help you achieve your personal or professional goals. I want you to think about this book as your personal toolkit, tool drawer or toolbox. You may only need to use one or two of these tools at any given time, but they're here to help you succeed now and in the future. Like your tools in your toolbox at home, the tools in this book have stood the test of time and never become obsolete. It makes no difference that these tools are not made of steel or wood. They are as essential to achieving your goals as the welding torch is to building a skyscraper.

Over time and with a little practice, you will learn the benefits of each success tool and intuitively reach for the one perfect for helping you get the job done efficiently with little or no resistance.

HOW TO USE THIS BOOK

This book is divided into three sections: "The Mindset of Success," "Support and Inspiration," and "Creating Success Habits." Each section will contain tools essential for achieving big goals and making positive change in your life. Each tool will be explained in detail. You'll understand what makes that tool so effective and why. There will be a practice exercise included with each tool. Here you'll be able to work with each tool in a fun and effective way. Also, I have included a brief writing exercise as well. Completing the writing portion will help reinforce your understanding of that tool and document your progress. All the writing assignments found at the end of each tool will also be found together at the end of the book. This way you will have them all in one place when you want to go back and practice. In addition, I have peppered this book with actual stories of people who have used these tools and accomplished great things.

All the practice and writing exercises are based on my 25-year success journey as well as my having coached and taught over a thousand people, many of whom have gone on to achieve their goals and made major positive changes in their lives.

Just like the welding torch or hand mixer, using any tool takes practice and these success tools are no exception. The more you practice, the better you'll be at using them. Some of the tools you'll find in the book will come naturally to you and feel like an old friend. Others may seem strange and different. Either way, they all work to create positive and lasting positive change, so dig in, have a leap of faith and enjoy the journey.

A great way to get the most out of this book is to

give it a thorough read through initially, relaxing and just enjoying learning about each tool. Then go back and practice each tool. Many of you will start at tool number one and go through them in the order in which they appear. Others will jump around, and some of you may choose to initially focus on one or two tools that feel right for the task your currently dealing with. Either way, they will help you change your life and reach your goals. Do what comes naturally, honor your rhythm and enjoy the process.

My one suggestion would be to work with tools 3, 4 and 5 in that order. These three tools are all connected in that they teach you how to change your thinking from negative to positive mindset. I have separated tools 3, 4, and 5 to give you a chance to digest and practice each one before moving ahead. Each one builds on the other so get the most out of this group by working with them one at a time. After a bit of practice, you will automatically combine them; you'll be able to notice a negative thought, stop it before it becomes a feeling, and substitute a positive one in its place. This will become as natural as breathing. This is key to achievement so trust me when I say this effort will change your life.

Other than that, there is no set order that you need to do the tools in for them to work and help you succeed.

The amount of time you spend working with each tool will also be your individual choice. You might choose to work with a tool for a day, a week or longer before moving on, it's up to you. You will know when it's time to move on. If you're not sure how much time to spend on each tool, let me suggest you try each tool for one week. Most people find that if they concentrate on one tool for a week, they develop mastery over it. Using a tool for a week also helps to commit it to memory, which in turn helps you to develop a new positive success habit.

Once you have used this book to help you achieve your go changes in your goal you'll find it a great reference book for future goals or changes. Many of you will keep revisiting and working with these tools throughout your lives. We all need tune-ups. If you have a period of uncertainty or feel your confidence wavering, come back and pick the tool that will put you back on track.

As I mentioned, accompanying each tool is a writing assignment in which I ask you to answer a few questions. Why not get a journal and keep all your writings in one place? Perhaps you can call it "My Success Journal" or any title you like. There is great power in writing and having a journal just dedicated to the success you will have working with this book. Writing is a wonderful way to reinforce your learning and remind you that your awesome and can do much more that you thought possible.

It is my greatest hope that you will enjoy this book and use it as a powerful ally in having what you always dreamed of. These tools have worked for thousands – I know they will work for you!

MINDSET

"THERE ARE NO LIMITATIONS TO THE MIND EXCEPT THOSE WE ACKNOWLEDGE. BOTH POVERTY AND RICHES ARE THE OFFSPRING OF THOUGHT." —NAPOLEON HILL

Mindset put simply is the way we feel or think about any given situation. Our mindset is a major determining factor in our success. In any venture or pursuit, be it personal, professional or spiritual, the way we think and feel about our ability to succeed will shape our outcomes. Every spiritual paradigm or self-help strategy acknowledges this. Negative thoughts and beliefs hold us back while positive ones advance us along the path to positive change.

This idea can be both empowering and troubling at the same time. Empowering because it's nice to believe we can think and believe ourselves into a winning outcome. After all, who among us doesn't have fantasies and daydreams about succeeding in our mission, if only for a moment. Troubling because for many of us we have not been able to accomplish what we want and that alone can make us doubt our abilities to change deeply held thoughts and beliefs. We might say to ourselves, "If my thoughts and beliefs help or hurt me, and I can't seem to go to that next level or get what I desperately want, what am I doing wrong? Why can't I control my mind, after all, it is mine." Don't worry you're not alone in these thoughts and help is on the way. Each tool in this section will gently but gradually help you shift your thoughts and beliefs from negative to positive. You will easily be able to consciously and subconsciously create and maintain a positive mindset.

11

TOOL #1 KNOWING YOUR "WHY"

> "HE WHO HAS A WHY TO LIVE
> FOR CAN BEAR ALMOST ANY
> HOW." —FRIEDRICH NIETZSCHE

This tool is an important first step in achieving your goal

Your "why" or as I like to call it "Y" is also your purpose for doing something. Being in touch with the reason or "Y" you want to achieve a goal or make a change in your life is the first step to accomplishing it.

Your "Y" is not the same thing as your vision or goal. The "Y" is more fundamental. It's the reason you want to do something and not the thing itself. Your "Y," or purpose, is the reason behind it all.

Being in touch with your purpose will be the engine that will keep you moving forward through the easy and rough patches of your journey. Setbacks or even failure may be part of your path to success. Being in touch with your "Y" will help you push through and not give up.

So how do you get in touch with your "Y?" The easiest way to do this is actually very simple, ask yourself. Why do I want to...........?

Your first answer may or may not be the underlying

"Y." We are like onions, we have layers upon layers of reasons for things. Try and get to the most fundamental reason you can. If your answer seems too superficial, keep asking the same question. Eventually you will get to the real underlying reason, or your "Y."

Not too long ago, a coaching client of mine, Robert, went to the doctor for an annual checkup. He knew he was a bit overweight, but thought it was no big deal. "What's 30 pounds?" he told himself. What he didn't know was that under the surface two threats were lurking, pre-diabetes and a potential stroke or heart attack due to high LDL or bad cholesterol. Now he had tried losing weight before and hadn't had much success. Like most people, he roller-coastered up and down 20 pounds or so. He decided then-and-there that he was going to release the extra 30 pounds and change his blood sugar chemistry to perfect levels. He also decided that he would do this through diet and exercise alone. He knew that for him to accomplish this, he would need a clear sense of purpose, or to have a strong "Y," so as to not quit when things got bumpy.

Long story short, he did make the changes necessary to accomplish his health goals. He lost the weight by changing his eating habits and doing moderate exercise. He walked 4 days a week for 30 minutes each time. He told me, "This time it felt natural and easy."

Sure, sometimes he wanted to revert to his old habits, but he didn't. This time he could stay the course. He had gotten in touch with his underlying "Y."

Robert's "Y" around dropping the weight and lowering his blood sugar became crystal clear to him; He did not want to have a stroke and be a burdeon to his family and he did not want to be on any medication, period. He believed that medication would lead to more severe complications and he wanted to avoid them. His "Y" for releasing this excess weight was to stay healthy for his family and avoid taking drugs.

It worked for him. By being in touch with his "Y" Robert was able to stay the course and make the changes needed to get healthy and avoid taking medication.

Robert's down the 25 pounds and his blood sugar is perfect. Now when Robert thinks about having a sugary snack, he remembers his "Y" and makes a different choice. That's the power of the "Y."

Your "Y" will be unique to you. Perhaps you want financial security, a healthier body, to have a deeper love connection with your partner, or a new supportive relationship. Maybe you want to start that business or write that book you know is inside you. Perhaps your "Y" is being able to be generous to the causes of people in your life. Whatever your "Y" or sense of purpose is, keep that foremost in your mind. Knowing and constantly remembering your "Y" will move you toward success.

PRACTICE IDENTIFYING YOUR "Y" OR THE PURPOSE FOR YOUR WANTING TO CHANGE

I want you to think about what it is that's motivating you to make this change in your life. What is behind your vision or goal? Why do you want what you want?

Write down your "Y," the underlying reason you want to achieve your goal. Now put your "Y" statement somewhere where you will see it every day. Perhaps your bathroom mirror or on your refrigerator. You decide, but put your "Y" somewhere visible where you will see it often.

WRITING EXCERCISE

› What is my "Y" statement?

› How does it feel being crystal clear about my "Y?"

› Where can I put this statement where I will see it often?

› How would I explain knowing your "Y" to someone who has not read this book yet?

GETTING CLEAR ON YOUR VISION OR GOALS

"IN ORDER TO CARRY A POSITIVE ACTION WE MUST DEVELOP HERE A POSITIVE VISION." —DALAI LAMA

This tool will help you understand the importance of setting goals

Visions and goals are similar. A vision may be thought of as your future self while goals may be broken down into tasks you will accomplish along the way to achieving your vision. Many people will consider a vision and a goal to be the same thing; that's OK. They are both a version of things not yet realized. In this tool, I will use the word vision and goals interchangeably.

Your vision is your mission, your end game, your ultimate goal. A vision is always a future version of life. Having a vision gives us a sense of purpose. Vision helps us to define our values and prioritize our lives. Having a clear vision will keep you going through good times as well as bad.

Having goals transforms the way we feel about ourselves. Now, with a goal in mind, we can see ourselves as more. A vision unlocks the wonder of possibility within us. As we become clear about our vision, we learn about ourselves, who we are and what truly matters. We begin to feel strong; we begin to believe in our ability to change in ways we never thought possible.

We are all familiar with the pattern of setting a goal, getting excited, and beginning to go for it. In the beginning, we have great energy and enthusiasm. Over time, however, that initial energy begins to dissipate. This is the time when many will give up. During these times, focusing on your goals will give you the motivation to continue. Your vision will keep you on track. Once over the hump, your renewed excitement and energy takes over once again.

Your vision gives you the impetus to work towards something every day. The ability to make steady progress (no matter how slow) towards your goals will keep you fired up and moving forward. It is only by having a goal or vision that we can measure our progress and celebrate our successes along the way.

Finally, having goals and visions will help us to live life to the fullest. If you want to continually feel the pride and self-confidence that comes with achieving meaningful things throughout your life, then having visions and goals will make that possible.

PRACTICE VISIONING AND GOAL SETTING

Over the course of the next few days begin to ask yourself, "What is it I want to accomplish?" If you have more than one goal, prioritize them. Which ones do you want to do first? What time frame will you want to accomplish them in?

WRITING EXCERCISE

› Write out your vision of yourself. Go into as much detail as possible.

› Why do I want this in my life?

› What goals will I need to accomplish to achieve my vision?

› Prioritize your goals in order of importance to you.

› How will my life change once I have achieved my goals/vision?

› How do you feel having gotten in touch with your vision/goals?

› Keep a daily record of what you have done to accomplish your goal, no matter how big or small.

› How would you explain the importance of goal-setting to someone who has not read this book?

In the next 3 tools, I'm going to teach you how to turn a negative thought into a positive one. I have divided this process into 3 parts. It's easier to master this process if you practice each part separately before you combine them. In no time, you'll be doing this naturally without giving it a second thought.

THE FLASHLIGHT

"UNTIL YOU MAKE THE UNCONSCIOUS
CONSCIOUS, IT WILL DIRECT YOUR
LIFE AND YOU WILL CALL IT FATE."

—C.G. JUNG

*This tool will help you develop awareness of your
subconscious negative thought patterns*

If you're feeling excited and nervous about your ability to mind your mind, to shift from a negative to a positive mindset, that's perfectly natural. Don't worry, you're not alone. This first tool will get you started making deep and permanent changes in the way you think. This tool is the first step in creating a positive mindset. You can't solve a problem unless you know what it is. This tool is going to gently make you aware of what's happening between your ears that you aren't even aware of.

Recent research in the field of neuroscience teaches us that we all have between sixty and seventy thousand thoughts each day. How many of those are we conscious of? Very few. It is this lack-of-awareness about our thinking habits that gets us into trouble... and we're going to begin to change this.

I'll wager that many of those 60,000 plus thoughts we have daily are negative and we don't even know it. It was for me and most of the people I have worked with over the years. In a way it's unavoidable. We have been programmed since childhood to think and focus on the bad rather than the good, the media, our families (well-meaning as they may be), work, as well as our social environments have all contributed to our negative mindset, our sense of doom and gloom.

Using this first tool, we will begin to develop an awareness of our thoughts and begin to dissolve our habit of thinking negatively. Dissolving negative thoughts will have the wonderful effect of allowing more positive thoughts to take their place. We're beginning to make the mental shift from a negative to a positive mindset. A more positive mindset will allow us to make the positive changes we seek.

The flashlight will help you become aware of what you're thinking about below the surface. In order to make positive changes in *the way* we think and feel, we must first get to know *what* we think and feel. Becoming aware of what we're thinking about all day is the first step required to make the shift from negative to positive thinking.

Look at it this way; if you are walking in the woods at night and you keep tripping over rocks and tree roots, it's most likely because you cannot see them. Even though you may want very much to stop tripping, if it's dark and you can't see well then you'll have no choice but to keep repeating this over and over. If, however, you bring a flashlight and shine a light on your path, something very different happens. Now, maybe for the first time, you see those rocks and roots clearly. The light allows you to walk safely and steadily around them without tripping.

Beginning to change to a more positive mindset works the same way. The flashlight will illuminate the negative thought patterns you are subconsciously stuck in, allowing you to become aware of and eventually avoid them. I love this tool because it's so easy to use and once you practice it you'll be changed forever. I promise!

A WORD OF CAUTION is needed at this point. Be gentle with yourself and don't judge yourself during this process. It's not about the number; it's all about the thoughts themselves.

PRACTICE EXERCISE: HOW TO USE THE FLASHLIGHT

For one week you are going to keep track of every single negative thought you have while you're awake. It's easy and fun if you follow my instructions.

REMEMBER ONLY NEGATIVE THOUGHTS FOR NOW!

Get a small pad you can keep in your pocket or bag, or start a new list or note on your smartphone. The main thing is that you can grab that pad and pen or phone in a second over-and-over without hassle. When I did this, I had a small flip up spiral pad and pen I kept in my backpocket.

Every time you have a negative thought about anything, make a note of it. Use a check, roman numerals or any way you want to keep track. A negative thought is anything that's not positive.

I remember when I first used this tool I was astounded how many negative thoughts I had on a daily basis. I did it for a full week and often I would have over 125 marks on my pad. That's totally normal so the more, the merrier. Remember, no negative self-judgement, just keep track.

In tools 2 and 3, you will learn how to quickly change those negative thoughts into positive ones.

Here are some examples of **negative thoughts:**

I hate this traffic

My job sucks

I'm so fat

She's such a jerk

I hate to do this

I know I'm going to screw it up

She'll never change

He doesn't get me

I'll never find a great job

I'll never lose this weight

I'm too old

I'm too sick

How am I going to pay for that?

I hate myself

No matter what the negative thought you have just make that check mark. If you notice you repeat the same negative though throughout the day, make another mark. What we're doing is shining a light on the number of negative thoughts we have each day, and not the thoughts themselves, so that we may notice as many as possible.

Each night add up all the marks and keep track of that number. Remember: the more, the merrier. This number just shows your growing level of awareness over your previously unconscious thought patterns.

DON'T JUDGE YOURSELF, COMPLIMENT YOURSELF AT THE END OF EACH DAY

At the end of each day, after you have added up all the marks and you can see how many negative thoughts you had, take a deep breath and compliment yourself for being great at keeping track.

Do not judge yourself negatively. Instead, pat yourself on the back and tell yourself, **"I did a great job of keeping track today."** The more ticks you have, the better; this is because you are becoming aware of your negative thought patterns. Remember, it's the act of keeping track of and developing awareness of your negative thoughts that's important. Keep a tally of the totals on a daily and weekly basis.

Answer these questions at the end of each day:

› What have I learned about myself from using this tool?

› How would I describe this tool to someone who has not read this book?

THE "RESET BUTTON" OR "CANCEL CANCEL"

> "DO NOT IMPRISON YOUR MIND
> WITH NEGATIVE THOUGHTS."
>
> —LAILLAH GIFTY ALITA

*This tool teaches you how to change negative thoughts
into positive ones when they happen*

RESET BUTTON

Wow! Congratulations, if you have done step one and taken it to heart you most likely realize that you have a huge number of negative thoughts running through your head. I know I sure did. You also know that this is not the mindset for success. You understand that you have to get rid of those thoughts and begin a shift to a positive "can-do" mindset in order to make the change you want in your life.

Every highly successful person I have ever coached or talked with says the same thing; they are aware of what they are thinking about and they make a conscious choice to focus on what they want and solutions rather than problems.

So what now? What do you do with this new-found awareness? What about all these thoughts? Good question. First of all, remember, the act of being more conscious of your thoughts and aware of your negative thoughts, in particular, is healing and transforming in itself. This newfound awareness now puts you lightyears ahead of where you were last week. No more tripping over the same old stones and tree roots, no more unconscious negative thinking. You see clearly now what is occupying your mind and you understand that your mindset, the way you think and feel about yourself at any given moment, is a huge factor in your ability to make those positive changes in your life. You're on your way.

Each one of us has the ability to reset our thinking. Our minds are very open to suggestion. These tools are all about taking control of what you're thinking and banishing negative thoughts. You are now becoming in charge. You're beginning to show yourself that you can do anything you set your mind to, even change the way you think.

Repeating to yourself "Cancel Cancel—this is not the reality I want," or hitting the imaginary "Reset button" and saying "reset," when a negative thought appears is a powerful way to dissolve these negative thoughts in real-time. When you begin to use this tool, it's likely that you will be having a lot of negative thoughts. This is perfectly normal. You're still the same person you were last week, you just have not changed your mindset yet. This will change as you work with the tools in this book, but for now, this is where you are at and this is what we're going to cure.

Since our thoughts affect our emotional state, be it positively or negatively and you will need a new posi-tive and winning emotional state in order to achieve your dream, it's important that you dissolve your negative thoughts as quickly as possible. We don't want any negative thoughts to hang around long enough to have a chance to create a nega-tive emotion within you. By using "Cancel Can-cel" or hitting that "Reset Button" at the instant a negative thought pops in your mind, you're telling yourself NO! I don't want that thought now. You're on your way to directing the show.

Be gentle with yourself and congratulate your-self often. Whenever you cancel or reset a nega-tive thought, be sure to do it gently and lovingly without any negative self-judgement. Rather than thinking, "Here I go again, I'm so negative." or "I'm hopeless." think "Good job, I noticed an-other negative thought and took the right action." or, "I did it again, I dissolved a negative thought." or "Wow! I love being in charge of what I'm thinking about, this is fun!" Remember you are creating a new habit, a new response to years of old thought patterns, so give yourself credit as often as you can and realize this will take some time. You will be surprised how quickly this shift from negative thinking to positive thinking will occur.

By consciously changing your thoughts from negative to positive, not only are you acknowledging that you don't want that negativity in your mind but you are also acknowledging you want a different life. This is the mindset that will carry you through any success you want, be it small or massive.

You are becoming the architect of your thoughts and feelings and you will eventually become the architect of your ideal life. All successful people think mostly about what they want and how to accomplish that.

PRACTICE EXERCISE: HOW TO USE
"CANCEL CANCEL" OR YOUR "RESET BUTTON"

For the next week, every time you have a negative thought say either, "Cancel Cancel—this is not my reality," or hit the "Reset Button" in your mind and say "this is not my reality."

WRITING EXERCISE

In your journal, answer these questions daily or weekly.

> › How did it feel using this tool?

> › What have I learned about myself from using this tool?

> › Why is it important to reset my negative thoughts?

> › How would I describe this tool to others who have not yet read this book?

THE REFRAME....SO WHAT DO I WANT INSTEAD OF WHAT I DON'T WANT?

"SOME PEOPLE GRUMBLE THAT ROSES HAVE THORNS; I AM GRATEFUL THAT THORNS HAVE ROSES." —ALPHONSE KARR

This tool is used to replace a negative thought with a positive one

Now that you have become aware of your negative thoughts, and taken an action to cancel that thought, it's time to go to the next and final step in this process of positive thinking, it's time to replace that thought with a better one. This tool is essential to success because thinking about what it is you do want is the key to getting it. As Henry Ford said, "If you think you can or think you can't either way you're right."

Thinking about what you want, creates a positive mindset. This mindset will become the foundation of your success and ability to have the life you always dreamed of. All successful people, no matter what it is they have accomplished, are crystal clear about what they want.

For most of us, when we begin to ask ourselves "so what do I want?" we may not immediately know, or the question itself may feel a bit strange or even stressful. Don't worry about this. As you work with this tool, it will get easier. Eventually, being able to substitute a negative thought with a positive one will become second nature and a great source of joy and comfort.

You will have many times throughout the day to practice this, and practice makes perfect.

We are not pretending that our life is perfect at this point. We are simply restating a negative into a positive. Here are a couple of examples:

From:

> I hate this traffic **DEEP BREATH** to "I love driving when the roads are clear and I'm moving quickly," or "I wish the roads were clear and I was cruising right now."

> This meeting is going to suck **DEEP BREATH** to "I wish this meeting would really stimulate me professionally."

> I hate my body **DEEP BREATH** to "I would love to have a strong, thin body," or "I can imagine how great I would feel being fit and healthy."

> My relationship sucks **DEEP BREATH** to "I would love a relationship in which I have more in common with my partner."

I feel so alone **DEEP BREATH** to "I would love to have a group of close friends I can really trust and have fun with," or "I can't wait until I have a few really close friends."

I'll never get the job I want **DEEP BREATH** to "I would love a job where I'm making lots of money and really helping others, where I am appreciated for my contributions and where I feel at home."

THE DEEP BREATH

Notice I have highlighted deep breath in every example? Taking a deep breath after each negative thought does two things. First, it helps to dissolve that negative thought; you may want to visualize in your mind as you take a breath and see that thought dissolving and disappearing, the deep breath coupled with your ability to visualize will work wonders.

Secondly, taking a breath is a way of centering you. It allows you the mental space and clarity to think about what it is you do want in that moment. The deep breath is the one of the one-two punch in reframing negative thoughts into positive ones. I would suggest you take a deep breath every time you have a negative thought before you think about what it is you do want.

During the day, build on what you have already been practicing from the previous two tools. Only this time after you cancel cancel or hit the mental reset button ask yourself, "So what do I want?"

Now go ahead and take your deep breath and gently insert that new positive thought about what you want. Try and do this every time you have a negative thought that you are aware of.

WRITING EXCERCISE

› What is the change I want most in my life now?

› Why do I want this change to happen?

› How will I feel once I have accomplished this?

› What will my life change once this happens?

› How did it feel using this tool?

› How has using this tool changed me?

› How would I describe this tool to someone who has not read this book?

TOOL #6

UNDERSTANDING THE EFFECT NEGATIVE AND POSITIVE INFLUENCES, INCLUDING FAMILY AND FRIENDS, HAVE ON YOUR ABILITY TO MAKE POSITIVE CHANGES AND REACH YOUR GOALS

"KEEP AWAY FROM PEOPLE WHO TRY TO BELITTLE YOUR AMBITION. SMALL PEOPLE ALWAYS DO THAT, BUT THE REALLY GREAT ONES MAKE YOU FEEL THAT YOU TOO CAN BECOME GREAT."

—MARK TWAIN

This tool will raise your awareness about how outside influences help or hinder your efforts to change

All successful people have at least one thing in common: They don't let the dream killers, the naysayers, the doubters, get inside their heads.

For us to achieve great changes or accomplish big goals, we must maintain a positive "can-do" mindset. We must primarily be in a state of mind where we believe we can accomplish our goals. Other people can either help or hurt us when it comes to maintaining this "can-do" mindset.

How many times have you been excited about something, asked a friend or family for their thoughts, only to have them be critical or worse downright negative? What often happens at that point? Well, for most people the wind begins to leave their sails. We can instantly go from enthusiastic and motivated to let down, demotivated, and sometimes even stopped in our tracks.

On the other side of this equation, if we take our ideas to a friend, family member, coach or colleague who is positive and genuinely wants us to succeed, then that person's positive support and encouragement become contagious. That person's positive attitude towards us helps us on our journey to accomplishing our goal. That person can be an ongoing source of inspiration, mentoring, and support. In short, that person becomes a tool in our toolkit for accomplishing our goal.

This is one reason why hiring a success or life coach is so helpful for people. Your coach's job is to support you and help you accomplish what it is you want to do.

PRACTICING UNDERSTANDING: THE EFFECT NEGATIVE AND POSITIVE INFLUENCES, INCLUDING FAMILY AND FRIENDS, HAVE ON OUR ABILITY TO MAKE POSITIVE CHANGES AND REACH OUR GOALS.

Over the next week or so, identify who in your life are positive influences and who are negative ones. Try not to judge them or yourself. At this point, you are simply making a list that shows your understanding of this tool. This list will become a tool in deciding who you want to use as a source of support and who you will avoid.

You don't have to unfriend or divorce those who end up in your negative column. You will simply make a conscious choice to avoid sharing your plans or goals with them and try as best you can to limit their negative effect on you while you're in this period of accomplishment and change. Appreciate them for the good part they play in your life and focus on the folks in your positive influence column for support and guidance.

WRITING EXCERCISE

› Make a list of people who are positive influences for you during this period of change.

› Make a list of people who are negative influences for you during this period of change.

› Write a brief description of why limiting negative influences and surrounding yourself with positive influences is important for your success during this period of change.

AFFIRMATIONS: HOW TO USE THEM SO THEY REALLY WORK

"AFFIRMATIONS ARE OUR MENTAL VITAMINS, PROVIDING THE SUPPLE-MENTARY POSITIVE THOUGHTS WE NEED TO BALANCE THE BARRAGE OF NEGATIVE EVENTS AND THOUGHTS WE EXPERIENCE DAILY." —TIA WALKER

This tool will explain what affirmations are and how to use them correctly for maximum results

Affirmations have been long touted as essential tools for achieving success and making big changes in your life. The idea behind these claims is, if you can see yourself as you want to be, you help accelerate that change. When repeating an affirmation, it's done as if you have already achieved your goal. The ideal version of yourself. For example, if you're looking to make a career change you might repeat, "I have the perfect job and I'm so happy," or "I now have my dream job." When you affirm what you have before you have it, you trick your mind into believing you have it, and that can create the mindset of attraction and persistence.

While this sounds great on the surface there is a problem. For affirmations to work, you must believe them. To repeat an affirmation that has not happened and may be a long way off can feel false and unbelievable. That discord you feel when you say something you know to be false can block the thing you want from coming.

There is a solution—a way of using affirmations where you state what you are wanting and have complete believability in what you're saying. You will have complete alignment with your affirmation.

Here's how it works. Let's say you want to double your income from the previous year. You definitely want to use every tool you can to support you in this worthy and achievable goal. Affirmations can be very helpful. Remember you need to have total believability for affirmations to work. Rather than saying over and over, "my income is doubled from the year before," or, "I love having twice as much money as I did last year," try "I know I will feel wonderful when my income is twice what I made the year before," or, "I am totally sure I will love having twice as much money as I had last year."

What we did was tell the truth. That we would feel great when... It's easy to say and believe how you might feel when you have achieved your goals. Not so easy to believe that you have already achieved them. For any affirmation put the phrase, "I know I'll love it when..." or, "I know I'll feel great when..." This is the key to using affirmations for success.

Make a list of 5 affirmations that directly relate to your goal.

Now modify that list to include phrases like:

> "I know I'll feel great when…"

> "I can't wait until…"

> "I'm going to really celebrate when…"

> "I'm really looking forward to…"

Now insert your affirmation after that initial phrase. The completed more believable affirmation might sound like:

> "I am so looking forward to earning twice as much as I made the year before."

Say this affirmation over and over as often as you can in the complete form. If you feel good and honest with yourself as you repeat it, then you know you're doing it right. If you still feel some dissonance, change the beginning until you have a statement that feels good.

As you repeat it, think about what your life will be like when you have reached your goal. Really let yourself daydream about it.

› Make a list of your top 3 affirmations using the correct beginning.

› How does it feel saying them?

› What's your believability factor when you say them?

› If one still feels a bit unbelievable, then change the beginning to make it more believable.

SEGMENTING

"SOMETIMES I NEED TO BREAKDOWN MY LIFE INTO SMALL BITE SIZE PIECES. IT'S EASY FOR ME TO ENVISION OR PRE-PROGRAM THE WAY I WANT THEM TO GO." —EVAN LACON

This tool will keep you focused on positive outcomes throughout your day

I first heard about this tool when I was doing research for a workshop I was teaching on financial success in New York City. I came across the work of Ester Hicks. Esther is a student and teacher of the *Law of Attraction*. Her work has inspired millions to believe they can affect the way life turns out by deliberately thinking and feeling a certain way. Programming your life by the way you think and feel would be a good description of the *Law of Attraction*. I started to use this technique, and the results were nothing short of miraculous. I started with seemingly small segments and soon found myself using it constantly throughout my day. It always works; I have never been disappointed!

For many people, it's too overwhelming or unbelievable to imagine life as they want it instead of how it actually is. Here's a tool that has the same effect of helping to create your ideal life but in bite-sized pieces. I love this tool and use it all the time.

Segmenting is the process of dividing your day into its many individual tasks. Examples are: a long drive or bus ride to visit a friend, a meeting, an interaction with colleagues, bosses or a loved one, a doctor visit, preparing a dish or meal, or sitting down to write a book. These are some of the many things that you do daily, and these are segments of your day.

In Segmenting, we begin to think of these segments as pre-programmable. Segmenting is when we consciously identify and focus only on a particular task and mentally see yourself completing that task with a positive outcome. The belief here is that we can influence the outcome of each segment by the way we think and feel about it before we do it.

By thinking about and focusing on the ideal outcome we want for that segment, we, in essence, are pre-programming its outcome.

If you're about to take a drive to meet a potential client, you may say to yourself, "I will arrive safely, refreshed and in a great frame of mine."

If you're heading into a meeting with a boss, you may say to yourself, "I will be pleasantly surprised by the results of my meeting, this meeting will be positive, and I will be happy with the outcome."

Perhaps if you're about to go on a date, you might say, "I am going to enjoy myself on this date regardless of the outcome."

Let's say you're heading to a doctor's appointment; you may say something like, "the results of this doctor's appointment will ultimately have a positive effect on my life."

In every example, the segment or task was identified and a positive outcome for that segment was visualized and spoken either out loud or to yourself prior to beginning it.

You will likely not pre-program all of your daily tasks, but certainly use this tool for those segments of your day in which you have a great investment in a positive outcome.

Segmenting is so powerful for creating a desired result that you'll want to use it often. Not only will your days be great, but also you will undoubtedly feel a sense of empowerment and spiritual connectedness as you become a deliberate creator of your life.

PRACTICING SEGMENTING

Think about the many tasks you will do today. Before each task, I want you to take a minute and decide the ideal outcome for that task. Once you have done this, state out loud or to yourself that positive outcome. Begin that task or segment. Once you have completed that task notice how close you are to having it turn out the way you stated it would. Celebrate that, now on to the next. And on and on throughout your day.

WRITING EXCERCISE

› Lisl 5 segments you identified today.

› For each segment write the ideal outcome you imagined.

› How close was the outcome to the one you preprogrammed?

› How is it feeling using this tool?

› I low would you doscribe Segmenting to someone who hasn't read this book?

DON'T OVERTHINK IT, ESPECIALLY AT NIGHT

"THINKING HAS MANY TIMES MADE ME SAD, DARLING; BUT DOING NEVER DID IN ALL MY LIFE."

—ELIZABETH GASKELL

This tool will help you not give into fear or false thinking

I don't know about you, but there have been many times where I have had to tell myself "stop thinking about this. I'm tired now, it's not real, and certainly not good for my state of mind." Being able to say this to myself and understand those negative thoughts for what they are and refusing to believe in them is the goal of this tool.

Overthinking is another term for doubting yourself. Thoughts of fear, worry and doubt are all byproducts of overthinking. Overthinking can lead to anxiety and depression and will most certainly derail us from our goals if allowed to flourish.

Overthinking is more likely to happen when you're not busy. Nighttime is notorious for overthinking. Being tired and not engaged in activities that keep you busy is when overthinking likes to rear its ugly head.

When you are embarking on a big goal, fear and uncertainty will naturally show up from time to time. This is your ego, or rational mind, protesting as you leave the familiar and comfortable areas of your life and begin pushing your boundaries to new and unexplored territory. Negative thoughts are your mind's way of saying "don't take a chance, do what you have always done, who knows what will happen if you do this." The rational mind will try and tell you these things even if what you have always done has not helped you to achieve your goals and in many cases, has kept you stuck. Overthinking or giving into negative self-talk will stop you in your tracks if you let it. In the words of William Shakespeare, **"Our doubts are traitors, and make us lose the good we might win, by fearing to attempt."**

Those who achieve success have these thoughts as well. The difference is that successful folks understand these negative thoughts for what they are, the ego's attempt to get back into familiar territory. Through this understanding, they can put them aside and move on towards their desired outcomes. People who achieve great things do not overthink things and give in to fear and doubt.

Now there are a couple of great ways to deal with the problem of overthinking. The first is super simple. When you find yourself mired in self-doubt and fear (for many this happens at night when they are done with the tasks of their day and lying in bed), take a few deep breaths, remind yourself that you're overthinking again. Don't judge yourself harshly. On the contrary, celebrate and acknowledge your growing awareness and insights by labeling these thoughts as overthinking. Gently tell yourself that it's nighttime, and this is not a good time to be thinking about such things. Remind yourself that you are more susceptible to negative thoughts at night and that these thoughts are not real. Finally, tell yourself that tomorrow morning things will seem bright and possible once again. You'll be amazed at how this dialogue can dissolve the negative thoughts resulting from overthinking.

Activity is one of the best ways to switch from negative to positive thinking. If you find yourself overthinking a situation during the day, try getting busy. Instead of allowing negative thoughts to take hold, find an activity to do. Any actions in furtherance of your goals will be a great antidote to overthinking. Doing anything positive will dissolve negative thinking and put you back in a state of "I can do this."

If you find yourself constantly overthinking, go back and work with tools two through four in this book. They will help you identify negative self-talk and replace them with thoughts that make you feel good and put you back on track. Over time these negative voices will lessen as you prove to your ego that you can, in fact, do new things and that you're not going to die as a result. Every time you experience success, you rewire your brain to allow more and more appropriate risk-taking and expansion.

PRACTICE NOT OVERTHINKING IT, ESPECIALLY AT NIGHT

When you find yourself overthinking, remind yourself that you're overthinking. Call it what it is. Do this in a self-loving and gentle manner. After all, your new insights are a sign of personal growth. If it's nighttime and you're lying awake in bed tell yourself "I'm not going to think about this now." Remind yourself that "It's nighttime, I'm tired, and if I'm still worrying about this in the morning when I'm awake I can think about it then." Now go to bed or distract yourself with something relaxing and fun. Read a book, watch TV or listen to music. Whatever is fun and will take your mind off your thoughts, do it.

If you find yourself overthinking throughout the day, use distraction and get busy doing something that is aligned with your goals. Your mind will not be able to obsess on the negative and concentrate on the positive thing you're engaged in at the same time.

If you want to sharpen your skills of reframing negative thoughts to positive ones, then reread and practice tools 2 through 4 at the beginning of this book.

WRITING EXCERCISE

› Keep an overthinking log over the course of a week and jot down when you find yourself overthinking.

› After a day or two of this, jot down what method you use to stop the overthinking.

› In your overthinking log, note any progress you notice regarding overthinking.

› Briefly describe this tool of not overthinking to someone who has not read this book.

SUPPORT & INPSIRATION

"EACH PERSON HOLDS SO MUCH POWER WITH-
IN THEMSELVES THAT NEEDS TO BE LET OUT.
SOMETIMES THEY JUST NEED A LITTLE NUDGE,
A LITTLE DIRECTION, A LITTLE SUPPORT, A
LITTLE COACHING, AND THE GREATEST THINGS
CAN HAPPEN." —PETER CARROLL

When we make the decision to change our lives, we are often full of excitement and optimism. In that moment, we are 100% convinced we can have what it is we want and we can do whatever it takes to get the job done. In that moment, we are in a positive mindset. We are inspired!

The problem is, as time goes by and life happens, we often lose momentum and become derailed from our goals. That excitement and can-do attitude we had seems like a distant memory. Sadly, we can't get back to that place of inspiration. Like New Year's resolutions, we have started and stopped or the many diets we have tried and failed. We start off strong and committed only to fizzle out. This is all too often how our dreams and goals for change get put aside. When this happens, we're the ones who lose—that new business venture falls flat or our dream of a fit and healthy body or a supportive and fun relationship disappear.

There is hope! It is possible for you to have what you want no matter what it is. You can begin strong and stay strong on your path to achieving your goal, even when things get tough. You can go further than you have ever gone before. You can stay inspired! The tools found in this section of Support and Inspiration will take you there.

By using these tools, you will be able to stay the course of change and succeed. Here we go.

TOOL #10   FIND YOUR SOURCE(S) OF INSPIRATION

"I DREAM MY PAINTING AND I PAINT MY DREAM." —VINCENT VANGOGH

This tool will help you identify your source(s) of inspiration

Inspiration can be found in many different places and it comes in many different forms. For one person, it can be attending a religious ceremony. For another it's reading or listening to a book or motivational speaker. Still others get inspiration from being in nature, while gardening, stroking a pet, cooking, chanting, meditation or lovemaking. People are different, so the sources of inspiration will be very individual.

Everyone experiences inspiration differently as well. For some it's a subtle knowing, others may get a strong idea or calling to take a action. Once we are open to receiving inspiration and begin to seek it out consciously, then it will come.

Trust becomes important here. Inspiration can often be subtle. Like a gentle push to take a certain action or a strong feeling about something you need to do next. Trusting in your inspiration will develop as you see the positive results you're getting to follow it.

Inspiration will always be positive and lead to a positive result. Sometimes you may be inspired to make a change in your life that may take you out of your comfort zone. Changes like that can feel a bit frightening. Especially when your goals are big and you're changing behaviors as well as beliefs in order to accomplish them. Often these big changes are necessary and lead us to get what we want.

If you already know what inspires you or where to find inspiration, that's awesome. This means that you know what it feels like to be inspired. You have felt that sense of guidance and excitement. You know what it's like to be "on the right track." You trust your inspiration.

If you have not yet had that experience of getting inspiration, don't panic. Everyone has been there. Here's what you do: The first step to finding inspiration is to ask for it. Yes, you heard me, just ask. But who do I ask, you may be thinking. Ask yourself. Take a moment, get quiet and in your mind's eye ask yourself to show you a source(s) of inspiration. If you already have a spiritual center, God or higher power, ask it. Once you ask, simply stay open. Be open to the feeling of being connected to something higher than yourself. Stay open to being guided. Notice when you may have a feeling of safety or a sense of guidance about what to do next. That's inspiration.

Asking for inspiration and being open to it is all you need to do. Once inspiration shows up, your job is to trust it and act in accordance with that guidance.

PRACTICING FINDING YOUR SOURCE OF INSPIRATION

For the next few days, consciously ask for your source(s) of inspiration to be revealed to you. Do this as often as you can remember to. Notice where or when you feel most inspired as if your prayers for inspiration are being heard and answered. Notice and trust any inspirational thoughts, feelings or calls to action you may receive.

WRITING EXCERCISE

› What did it feel like asking for your sources of inspiration to be revealed to you?

› Where and when did you most feel a sense of inspiration?

› What did that inspiration feel like?

› What is your level of trust in your feelings of being Inspired?

› After a few days do you notice a change in your belief about being inspired?

› What is it you want most in your life right now?

› Why do you want this change to happen?

› How strong is your desire for this change to happen?

› How would you describe the tool of locating your source(s) of inspiration to another person?

TOOL # 11 CREATE A POSITIVE SUPPORT SYSTEM DURING THIS PERIOD OF BIG CHANGE

"SURROUND YOURSELF WITH ONLY PEOPLE WHO ARE GOING TO LIFT YOU HIGHER." —OPRAH WINFREY

This tool will reinforce why it is essential to your success to create a support system and how to do that

The support and encouragement of others you trust and admire can make all the difference in you achieving your goals. As discussed previously in tool number six you may have already made a list of potential support people. Remember, it is essential that you have at least one consistent source of encouragement and support while you're making big positive changes in your life.

Support can come in two varieties: emotional support and practical support. Emotional support will help you to deal with the emotional issues that are likely to arise as you stretch yourself and grow. Emotional support is more along the lines of having a supportive shoulder to lean on.

Practical support on the other hand, is support for taking actions. Unlike emotional support, practical support is about action and accountability. You will undoubtedly be taking many actions to accomplish big things. Having someone to share them with is very helpful. Examples would be a regularly scheduled check-in call with a coach, an action partner or another person who's willing to hear about the tasks you're planning to take on as well as the ones you have completed. This can be a short daily or weekly call taking 5 minutes or less or something longer; you decide what's best for you. These calls are great for getting us in the mindset, "I AM GOING TO DO THIS NO MATTER WHAT." The main point here is having a consistent person(s) to support you and hold you accountable during this time.

By telling someone what you're planning on doing that day, you are holding yourself accountable for doing it. What a great motivator!

Hiring a professional coach. If you can afford it, can be a great decision. Accomplishing big goals requires alot of positive support. It's hard to become great on your own! A professional coach can help. Coaches are trained to guide you, support, and hold you accountable for your successes and setbacks along the way. Coaching is a powerful tool for keeping us moving forward.

I hired a success coach a few years ago. I wanted to double my income from the year before and I felt

I needed that high level of professional support to accomplish what I was trying to do. I knew it would be hard but I didn't want to quit before I reached my goal. It was a short term agreement in which we skyped once a week for 4 weeks. It was really awesome. The experience did support me in reaching my financial goal. Just as important though, I learned a lot about myself from that experience as well. I recommend coaching if you can.

Choose wisely, for being open and vulnerable can be risky. You want to make sure your openness is always met with love, encouragement, and support. Professionals are trained to be supportive and encouraging, find one you feel great about.

It is not necessary to hire a professional, however. Maybe you can't afford a professional coach or are not comfortable sharing with a stranger; that's ok. Your success team can include people from your family, spiritual community, professional associates, and even virtual persons such as motivational entrepreneurs or healers.

The main criteria for being part of your support team is that these people genuinely want you to succeed, and they have experienced success themselves.

Your support can be in the form of a mentor. Someone who has already gone beyond where you're at.

Someone who is willing to teach you. Maybe it's someone who already has what it is you want, or someone who has great knowledge and skills in a related area. The key is to be able to learn and grow from this person(s). Always be moving forward towards where you want to end up. Try as best you can to get ongoing knowledge from people who have done it already. Find people from whom you can gain strength and understanding along the way.

Putting together your support system can be a fun and easy process. Remember, your support system can be as few as one or as large as you feel helpful. There's no right size of a support team; it's really up to you. You may change your support team during your journey as well. People's ability to be there for you may change. One member of your team who initially was available for daily or weekly check-in calls may no longer be able to do that. In cases like this don't get discouraged, find another person. The main thing is to keep yourself supported.

What you want in your support system are people who are willing and available to be there for you during your journey of change and growth, or while you're accomplishing a specific goal. The best way to get this going once you have chosen whom you want is to ask them. Simple as that. Tell them what you're doing. Let them know that you will most likely need some support and encouragement along the way. You can tell them that you thought of them because they have the skills, success or whatever you feel would really help you, especially if things get bumpy. Then ask them. It can be as simple as that. Most people will feel honored and glad to help you.

IF you are going to hire a professional, do your homework, find the best person for your budget and you are good to go.

PRACTICE DEVELOPING AND USING A SUPPORT SYSTEM

Decide if you want your support team to be professional, nonprofessional or both. If you're hiring a success or life coach, do your research and find someone you feel good about and get that started. For the non-professionals, decide who has the personality and experience you feel would be a great source of support for you. Ask them.

Give yourself a huge hug and tell yourself GOOD JOB! Recognizing the need for support and asking for it or hiring it, is a huge self-loving, self-investing act. You're saying to yourself, "I WILL SUCCEED AT ANY COST." I'm so proud of you, and you should be proud of yourself too.

› Make a list of your support team.

› How did you feel when you realized you needed a support system?

› How did you feel asking for people to be on your support team?

› What were their reactions like when you asked them to be on your side?

› How would you explain this tool to someone who has not read this book?

› What is the difference between emotional and practical support?

I
CREATING
SUCCESS
HABITS

"WE ARE WHAT WE REPEATEDLY DO. EXCELLENCE THEN IS NOT AN ACT, BUT A HABIT." —ARISTOTLE

A habit is nothing more than something we do over and over again. "According to scientific research, on average it takes 66 days to form a new habit." —Researchers from University College London.

This section is all about developing new success habits that will support you in your success journey and achieving new goals. Neuroscience will be very helpful here in understanding how habits are formed and the way the brain works in helping us to grow in massive ways. Also, behavioral science gets a nod as well. Habits, those things we do over and over again, are the key to us making changes in our lives. Whether the changes we are seeking are small, large, or massive, developing and using new habits will be key in getting what you want.

In this section, I will share with you some of the most powerful habits essential in accomplishing major positive change. These are the habits that highly success-ful people in all walks of life use. The more positive life-changing habits you can adopt, the faster and more permanent your success will be.

TIME MANAGEMENT
& THE TIME LOG

"THIS TIME, LIKE ALL TIMES, IS A VERY
GOOD ONE, IF WE BUT KNOW WHAT TO
DO WITH IT." —RALPH WALDO EMERSON

This tool will help you find the time to accomplish your goals

According to *Wikipedia*, time management "is the act or process of planning and exercising conscious control over the amount of time spent on specific activities, especially to increase effectiveness, efficiency or productivity."

Admittedly, the topic of time management is huge. For our purposes, however, I want to introduce you to one of the most powerful time management tools that has helped thousands to find and use the time needed to make big life changes.

The Time Log is a tool that has three purposes. First, it helps us to become clear on how we spend our time. Secondly, it helps us to find the additional time we will need to achieve our goals and thirdly it creates awareness around us spending enough time to accomplish what we want.

Time vagueness is when you have no idea where the time went. We've all been there. For most of us, this is not a huge problem because we know what we must do on a daily basis and get it done. Our days are structured and familiar, so that we make it to work on time, pick up the kids, are around for our favorite television show or other things we do regularly. Sure, we may want more time, but for the most part, we get done what we need to do.

The problem arises when we want to make a big change or achieve a large goal that will require more time. How do we carve out the extra time? The time log will help us do just that. Here's how it works. In order to find more time or reallocate time for a new endeavor, it is crucial to know how you spend your time. Becoming clear on exactly how your time is used each hour and day is the first step in becoming clear.

Your time log is a like a day planner only with 15-minute increments. Download or buy a planner that has this format so you can plug your activities into each slot. Below is an example I created in google docs. You can buy a planner or make your own as well. You will want to include every activity up until the time you go to sleep.

EXAMPLE TIME LOG

Day_____

Time in 15-minute increments

7:00 am _____ Make Coffee _____

7:15 am _____ Walk the dog _____

7:45 am _____ Shower and dress _____

8:00 am _____ Drive to work listening to an ebook for
_____ increased learning _____

9:00 am _____ Check in call with my support person ___

9:45 am _____ Meeting _____

10:00 am _____ Check Facebook _____

10:45 am _____ Working on the report for sales _____

11:00 am _____ Working on my project _____

11:15 am _____ Working on my project _____

11:30 am _____ Working on my project _____

12 noon _____ Fill in _____

12:15 pm _____ Fill in _____

12:30 pm _____ Fill in _____

Of course, the weekends will look very different than the weekdays. I would suggest you keep this log for one week.

What will happen is that you will begin to see exactly how you spend your time each day. For most people this can be very enlightening. Many of my coaching clients who I encourage to use this tool tell me just how surprised they are about how much time they spend doing things they hadn't given much thought to in the past. Activities like watching TV, surfing the Internet, and using social media are a few such examples.

Remember the purpose of this exercise is to create clarity about how you spend your time. Clarity is the necessary first step in setting aside time on a regular basis to use for your new goal.

Be gentle on yourself. No getting down on yourself, no beating yourself up for wasting too much time on *Facebook* or on the phone with your friends. Instead, I want you to pat yourself on the back for keeping this time log and becoming clear. Your willingness to do this is awesome and you are now in a position to shift the way you use your time to accommodate those tasks that will move you closer to your goals.

Now that you have kept your time log for the week, I want you to study it without self-judgement. Notice how you spend your time. Do you see a pattern? Maybe you spend alot of time doing things that are fun but not productive. Maybe you realize that you're not spending time on something you want or need to do. Once you begin to develop an awareness of how you are spending your time, you'll be amazed at what happens. As if by magic, you naturally begin to shift the way you spend your time. Especially if you have a strong "Y" for achieving your goal, you begin to want to do less of those things that use up too much time and don't move you towards success and more of those activities that will.

Just like with the Flashlight tool, clarity is the first step to making meaningful and lasting changes. In this case, in the way you use your time.

Now the second part of using the Time Log is to consciously make time for activities you want to do. Use a few blank time sheets and insert those activities you want to do in time slots that may have been otherwise used for less productive activities. Start slow; a half hour or 90 minutes can be a good start. Over time, you will naturally begin to use your time more productively and this process will feel very natural.

PRACTICE USING THE TIME LOG

For the next week, I want you to keep a time log. Keep track of exactly how you spend your time from when you wake up to when you go to bed. No gaps. Examine your time log daily and gently observe how you spend your time. NO JUDGEMENT, NO SELF-CRITICISM. Always congratulate yourself at the end of each day for keeping your log. Don't worry if you don't do it perfectly, over time you will.

WRITING EXCERCISE

› What did you learn about your use of time from keeping your log?

› How do you feel as you gain clarity over your use of time?

› What productive activities are you doing enough of?

› What unproductive activities are you doing too much of?

› How much time can you re-allocate for more productive activities?

› What activities would you like to do more of that will help you achieve your goal?

› How much time can you devote to those positive activities beginning now?

› How would you describe the Time Log to someone who has not read this book?

THE WILL DO LIST

"TODAY I WILL DO FOUR THINGS
TOWARDS MY GOAL." —EVAN LACON

*This tool will help you be consistently productive
and in control as you reach your goal*

The first thing I want you to understand is that the WILL-DO list is not the same as the TO-DO LIST. They differ in one huge and critically important way. The will-do list is a list you will make daily of tasks which are necessary for your reaching your specific goal and which you commit to doing the following day. The to-do list is comprised of tasks of a more general nature that you plan on doing but without a hard and fast deadline. While the to-do list keeps growing the will-do list is cleared out every day.

Every one of us has made to-do lists. These are lists of things we plan on doing the next day or sometime soon. The problem is, often these lists grow and grow as we keep adding new tasks but don't complete ones already on the list.

To-do lists can be a good organizing tool; however, for us to achieve a big goal we need to take consistent, productive action daily. The will-do list consists of only those actions directly related to that goal which you are pursuing, and you commit to completing each action by the following day. Keep your will-do list to a manageable number of tasks. 3 to 6 tasks is a good number to include on a daily basis. The main thing is that you complete every task on that list by the following day.

Now at this point, you may be thinking, "what if I look at my list today and realize that's not a necessary task," or, "what if it takes more than one day to complete?" Occasionally, you may have a task on your list that turns out to not be as important as you thought, or you start it and realize it's not what you want to do. In those cases, get rid of it.

When you're making your list for the next day, only include those talks on your will-do list which you believe are needed and will move you closer to accomplishing your goal. After a short time using this tool you will naturally become great at curating what tasks need to be included in your will-do list. Remember, the reason this tool is so effective in helping you achieve your goals is because you have the intention of completing everything on it the following day. You become highly productive.

Sometimes you will include a task that takes longer than one day to complete. In this case, include that portion of that task you will complete the following day. "I will do all the research needed to write my blog post," or, "I will write the first 5 sections of the productivity report I need to complete by Friday." Get the picture? Your goal is to do everything on your list the following day.

The will-do list becomes an accountability tool to keep you doing what you say you will, all the while moving closer and closer to achieving your goal. Your confidence, sense of self-control, and productivity will soar in no time.

PRACTICING THE WILL DO LIST

Beginning this evening, start your will-do list. On a pad, write down at least 3 but up to 6 actions you can commit to completing by the end of tomorrow. Do this every day you plan on working on your goal. If you take a day off, that's fine. Your list will begin the evening before you begin work again.

Every day check off the tasks as you complete them. Pat yourself on the back and congratulate yourself every eve when you see your completed list.

› Make your daily will-do list.

› Cross off each action once you have completed it.

› How did I feel today using this tool?

› What kinds of things can I include or exclude from this list to better reach my goal?

› How would I explain this tool to someone looking to reach a big goal?

STAY CONNECTED TO YOUR SOURCE OF INSPIRATION AND USE THAT GUIDANCE OFTEN

"WHAT I NEED IS SOMEONE WHO WILL MAKE ME DO WHAT I CAN."

—RALPH WALDO EMERSON

This tool will keep you inspired and moving forward toward your dreams and goals

In the tool, Finding Inspiration, you got in touch with your sources(s) of inspiration. You learned that asking for guidance and staying open to it is all you need to do to receive inspiration. Now it's time to make seeking inspiration a regular habit. Whatever you do to gain inspiration, I want you to do it often and on a regular basis. Remember you're trying to change your life in a big way. Like any big change, you must develop new habits that support change. Doing things the old way will keep you getting the old result. We don't want that. Massive action and positive change require new positive habits.

Whatever you discovered as inspiring to you that's what you need to incorporate regularly into your routine, especially during this period of positive change and growth. It's easy to lose steam and slip back into habits that do not foster new goals. Staying connected to your sources of inspiration is key in keeping the momentum going. Whether it's listening to books on tape, exercising, cooking, meditation, be-ing in nature, chanting, attending workshops and seminars, being with a beloved pet, or spending time praying, just set the intention to do it every day or at least 6 out of 7 days each week until you have reached your goal or made the changes in your life you want to make.

Practice staying connected to your source of inspiration, staying open to that help and using the guidance often.

How often should you do that? Until you have reached your goal, pick at least one thing that inspires you and do it daily or at least 6 out of 7 days each week. This habit of being open to and receiving inspiration will help you on so many levels. Inspiration is like the fuel that keeps our engine of change and growth going.

Daily inspiration helps to dissolve depression and feelings of isolation.

Remember this list and what inspires you will often change throughout your life. Let that change happen. If something new shows up that helps you to feel inspired, great, go with it.

If you are a journal writer, keep a daily inspiration log of what you did to be inspired and what inspiration you received.

PRACTICING STAYING CONNECTED TO YOUR SOURCE OF INSPIRATION AND USE THAT GUIDANCE OFTEN.

I want you to think about what inspires you. What makes you feel guided? What or who keeps you in a state of "I CAN DO THIS?" What gives you the momentum to keep going? Make a list of your sources of inspiration.

Now that you are clear on what you can do to get inspired, make a commitment and begin to incorporate doing at least one thing daily that inspires you. You can do more than one but the main thing is to do at least one inspiring activity daily, so you get into the habit of seeking and receiving inspiration. This habit will help you in this period of change and growth as well as throughout your whole life.

As always, be gentle with yourself and congratulate yourself for getting clear on your source(s) of inspiration.

> › What inspires me?

> › What inspiring activities am I doing regularly?

> › What inspiration did I receive from that activity?

> › How often am I doing them?

> › How does it feel incorporating inspirational activities into my daily routine?

> › What changes if any am I noticing as a result making inspirational activities a habit?

> › How would I describe this tool of staying connected to my source of inspiration to another person?

REGULARLY USE YOUR
SUPPORT SYSTEM, ESPECIALLY
WHEN TIMES GET TOUGH

"YOU CAN DO ANYTHING AS LONG AS
YOU HAVE THE PASSION, THE DRIVE,
THE FOCUS, AND THE SUPPORT."

—SABRINA BRYAN

*This tool will give you suggestions on
you how to use your supports*

Now that you understand how important it is to be supported while you're achieving your goals, let's talk about what the practice may look like. There's no right way to stay supported because everyone is different. You may go through periods where you need support, that's normal. As you reach out and get support regularly, you will most likely develop a sense of when it's time to make that call. The more you use your support system, the more you will come to appreciate them and feel the benefits.

One benefit of being supported is the feeling that you are not alone. For many high achievers, loneliness and isolation can set it. After all, what you are accomplishing may be very different from your old life and the lives of your friends and family. You may choose not to share much of your life during this period with them to stay in the "CAN DO" mindset. This is normal. Your support system will fill that gap. They will help you to feel connected and loved.

You don't have to have every answer, you don't have to feel up all the time and it's normal to have periods of fear and doubt. Therefore a support system is so essential to achieving your goals, with the right support you'll feel the pressure being lifted, and be able to move forward once again.

You may find it helpful to set up a regular "Action Call." This is a daily or weekly call with your support person to go over those actions you plan to take in that day or week. An action call is great for keeping you accountable. Telling someone you will do something is a powerful motivator for getting it done.

Other times you may need more emotional support. In those times, reaching out without any set schedule may feel right. The main thing is to establish the habit of getting support.

In the case of using a professional person such as a coach, trainer, teacher or therapist, you will likely have a set scheduled appointment time in which you will be able to talk about anything you need.

If you're hiring a professional, it's time to pull that trigger and get that started.

If your supports are non-professional, reach out to your supports and ask their permission to be one of your support people and gain their consent.

During the next few days, weeks or months, use one or more of your supports on a regular basis.

WRITING EXCERCISE

› List those people who are your supports.

› How does it feel having a support team?

› Write about a time you used your support person.

› What was the result of using that person for support, how did that change you?

› Now that you have experience with a support network, do you feel you need to make any changes to your network? If so, what changes would you make?

› How is your support network affecting your ability to reach your goal?

HAVING AN ATTITUDE OF GRATITUDE

"WHEN I STARTED COUNTING MY
BLESSINGS MY WHOLE LIFE TURNED
AROUND."—WILLIE NELSON

*This tool helps us remain positive and
stay in the mindset of success*

Few things can help us to feel good like counting our blessings. The more we acknowledge what we are grateful for, the happier we feel and the more confidence we have in our abilities. Many of us have gotten into the habit of thinking about what we don't have, what we're missing. This sense of lack can easily become our dominant mindset. We know this because if we are overly focused on what we don't yet have we feel badly. When this happens, it's because our thoughts are unbalanced and negative.

While wanting more is certainly a great motivator for growth and change, it is essential to balance that energy with an appreciation for what you have now that's good in your life. This balance of desire and appreciation will leave you feeling positive about yourself, hopeful about the future and determined.

Now gratitude is a mindset and could easily be located in the mindset section of this book. I put it here under habits because practicing gratitude is an easy habit to get into and one that is key to your accomplishing your goals.

Getting into the habit of reminding yourself of what you are grateful for is what we are going to accomplish here.

PRACTICING HAVING AN ATTITUDE OF GRATITUDE

Every day make a list or simply say to yourself at least three things you're grateful for. Use whatever tool you need to remind you to do this.

I have a client who keeps a "Gratitude Journal." In this journal, she writes down things she's grateful for throughout the day. She loves to look back and remind herself how fortunate she is.

I put an alert on my phone which pops up every evening and is titled "Gratitude List." This reminder helps me to stop what I'm doing, take a couple of seconds, reflect on my day and think of three things I'm grateful for.

Whatever works for you is great. The main thing is to become aware of at least three things you're grateful for every day. In no time, you will be developing the wonderful and transformational attitude of gratitude.

> How did it feel thinking about 3 things you were grateful daily?

> What tools are you using to remind yourself to do this daily?

> How has becoming grateful changed the way you think and feel about yourself and your life?

> How would you describe this tool "Developing an Attitude of Gratitude" to others?

GET COMFORTABLE WITH BEING UNCOMFORTABLE

"UNCOMFORTABLE = GROWTH AND GROWTH = SUCCESS." —OLIVIA JOHNSON

Learn how to deal with the discomfort that can arise as we grow and reach our goals

Every single person who has achieved success in any area of their lives will tell you that they have had to become comfortable with being uncomfortable. I would say this is a universal truth of achievement and success. The path to success will undoubtedly take you out of your usual realm of experience and cause you to think and act in different ways. Change can make us feel uncomfortable. It's a paradox of sorts that we need to change and grow to change and grow. Thus, we need to allow the feeling of being uncomfortable and appreciate that feeling as a sign that we're on the right track. This is a good thing, if you only did the same things you always did then you would be the same person you always were.

Becoming comfortable with being uncomfortable isn't always easy. I remember how I felt the first few times I gave live sales training workshops for a client who hired me to train their sales teams. While I had a great deal of sales training experience doing one on one or Webinar trainings, I hadn't had much experience doing live training workshops at that point in my career. I felt nervous and uncomfortable. I knew that I was going to do my job despite my feelings of discomfort. Why? Because I knew that doing those trainings was the next step towards accomplishing my ultimate goal of being a highly effective success trainer and coach.

How to get through the feelings of discomfort? There is no magic bullet here. The way you will be able to do what you need to do despite feeling uncomfortable is by trusting in two things: 1. You're doing what you need to do will bring you one step closer to your goal. 2. The world is not going to end if things don't go exactly the way you plan or hope.

Every time you do a difficult task so many great things happen: your skills improve, you become more self-confident, and your faith in your ability to reach the finish line becomes that much more certain. Get support if need be from your support system. There is no growth without change so keep that thought in mind and you'll be able to push through.

The second thing to keep in mind is that the world is not going to end if things don't go exactly the way you hoped. You're not going to die or be put in jail, and your life will continue. Tell yourself, "Life is for learning and no matter what happens I will learn from my experience." The benefits of taking the next right action towards your goal will far outweigh the possible discomfort of things not going perfectly.

PRACTICE FEELING COMFORTABLE AND BEING UNCOMFORTABLE

I want you to make a list or remember in your mind three things you have already done that were life-changing. They could have been things you recently did or in your past. Now remember how you felt prior to doing each one of those things. Now think about how you felt having completed them.

Over the next few days think about the actions you plan on taking towards your goal, I want you to get in touch with your discomfort level prior to taking each action and after you've completed it. In the cases where things go well, congratulate your-self and celebrate your success. If things don't go as you wanted, look for the silver lining. Ask yourself, "What can I learn from this experience?"

› What actions did I recently take towards my goal?

› How comfortable or uncomfortable was I before taking each action?

› How did I feel upon completing each action?

› What did I do or say to help me start those actions I was most uncomfortable with?

› Write a short statement on why it's important to become comfortable with being uncomfortable.

DEVELOP A HABIT OF LIFELONG LEARNING

> "LEARNING IS A TREASURE THAT WILL FOLLOW ITS OWNER EVERYWHERE."
>
> —CHINESE PROVERB

This tool will keep you inspired, growing and always moving forward in your life

Lifelong learning is just that, a habit of always learning something. When we learn, we grow, our brains expand and we stay relevant and useful to ourselves and others. As you set out to achieve a big goal, you will undoubtedly need to keep learning. Maybe you'll need to learn the technical aspects of your goal, maybeyou will need to acquire a new set of skills, or maybe you will need to keep learning how to stay positive and motivated. In any case, growing means learning.

Learning will inspire and support you as you move towards your goal. You can't do it alone. Learning will be an important source of support and inspiration. The gifts you get from learning are incalculable. Throw in a CD of someone who has what you want or is doing what you want to be doing and you will realize that it's possible. In addition, you will be receiving the wisdom from that person as if they were there with you on a one-on-one basis. What you do with that wisdom will be up to you. Investing in yourself via regular learning will create higher self-esteem, increased motivation, and greater persistence.

I remember when I was in a sales job in the mortgage business years ago. I had the goal of being the top producer in that office of over 50 Loan Officers. I set my intention on that goal and was open to all the inspiration and means necessary to achieve it. I already knew the business, so I felt that my mindset was what I needed to change. I decided until I reached my goal I would focus on having the mindset of a winner. Over the next 6 months, on my way to work, I listened to motivational books on tape on subjects that felt right for me. My commute was 45 min. I committed to creating the habit of listening to motivational tapes on my way to work and on the ride home. I allowed myself to listen to music or talk on the phone. By doing this I knew I would be learning daily for at least 45 minutes

I gained new skills that created more success at work. For example, I learned different techniques for closing sales I was not aware of and had not previously used.

Within 4 months of beginning this habit, I became the #1 most profitable Loan Officer out of 54 people in my organization.

I realized then, that for me to keep achieving more and having the life I wanted, I would have to incorporate regular inspirational messages and learning into my life on a regular basis.

In addition to the traditional forms of learning such as seminars, classes and workshops, we're lucky to live in a time when learning comes in other easily accessible forms such as eBooks, Books on tape, CDs, webinars and podcasts. I want you to make learning something a habit. When you're setting out to achieve a big goal like you are, learning regularly will be one of the tools most needed on your journey. You must continue to grow intellectually and spiritually if you are to change and grow in big positive ways.

Now learning doesn't have to be grueling lasting hours and hours a day. How much time you spend learning will depend on you. You may create a learning time on a daily basis, or you may wing it. Your goal will determine how long and how frequent your learning sessions need to be. As with every one of the tools in this book, BE GENTLE ON YOURSELF! Use this tool in a way that feels right for you. Have the courage to be honest with yourself and ask, "Is this moving me towards my goal in a way I want it to?" If not, make changes. You will know if you are doing it perfectly or need to make adjustments. The important thing is that you embrace the idea that continued learning is a powerful tool for positive change.

PRACTICING THE HABIT OF CONTINUED LEARNING.

I want you to think about what your goal is. Now think about what specific ongoing learning or inspirational material would help you reach that goal. Once you have identified what it is you want to learn first, go for it. Set up a routine of learning from that source on a regular basis. If you feel after a few days that you need to make a change in what you're learning, do it. It's natural as we grow and get closer to our goals that the learning or inspiration will change. Keep in touch with your feelings and make any adjustments needed along the way.

WRITING EXCERCISE

› What materials do I want to begin using for my regular learning?

› How often will I use them?

› After a few days, how am I feeling as a result of my ongoing learning?

› How would I describe this tool to someone who has not read this book?

TOOL #19   PERSISTENCE

"NOTHING IN THE WORLD CAN TAKE THE PLACE OF PERSISTENCE. TALENT WILL NOT: NOTHING IS MORE COMMON THAN UNSUCCESSFUL MEN WITH TALENT. GENIUS WILL NOT: UNRE-WARDED GENIUS IS ALMOST A PROV-ERB. EDUCATION WILL NOT: THE WORLD IS FULL OF EDUCATED DERE-LICTS. PERSISTENCE AND DETERMI-NATION ALONE ARE OMNIPOTENT."

—CALVIN COOLIDGE

*This tool will be the engine that will
power you reaching your goals*

No matter what your goal is, you will need to put continued, persistent effort in if you want to achieve it. So many people have a dream, get excited, and begin the work needed to get there only to fizzle out. All of a sudden, they sit down to work and have an unquenchable need to organize their closets. Or they decide to take a day off from the tasks needed to win. That day becomes two days and then three; before they know it they're no longer working towards their goals and dreams.

Persistence is the only cure. Every successful person I know will tell you that they persistently work towards their goals. It's a universal truth.

You must use all the tools in the book to keep persistently working toward your goals. Persistence is a habit. One that you must develop to succeed at something big. Like any new habit, the first few days are the most crucial. Once a month or two of continued effort have passed, working on your goal will feel much easier and can even become a habit you find you can't live without.

When I set out to write this book, I had not been in the habit of writing regularly. I know that for me to do this in the 12 weeks I had to develop a habit of writing regularly. I settled on a habit of writing 3 hours a day at least 6 days a week. After a few days of that, I realized that 3 hours was too long. Sure, some days I worked for three hours but on others, I became tired and mentally exhausted after 2pm. What I did was adjust my expectations to writing on average two hours a day. I was in the beginning stages of developing a habit of writing and knew I had to find a daily writing routine that worked for me that I could stick with.

Now, in the beginning, there were days I felt lazy and didn't want to go into my office and write. That's where my support and inspiration network came in handy. I could make a call to one of my action partners (see tool: Use your support system as often as you need, especially when times get tough). And by stating to her what I needed and intended to do that day, I was committed. The point here is that I committed to doing whatever it took to persistently work toward my goal of writing this book in 12 weeks. Sure enough, by week 5, writing daily became a habit I looked forward to. I had created a Success Habit.

Without persistence, I never would have gotten to that point.

PRACTICING PERSISTENCE

Think about your goal. Ask yourself, "What actions do I need to take on a regular basis to reach my goal?" Now make a list of those actions, prioritizing them in order of importance. Now commit to doing the first most important action on your list starting today. Commit to doing it until you've reached your goal.

Begin with one thing at a time. Don't try and do everything all at once. Prioritize your action list. Based on your goals. For me, to write this book, I knew that the first most important action I had to take was getting into the habit of writing daily. I started with that and did not incorporate any other behavior or mental learning actions until that pattern was well established.

Being persistent in taking the necessary actions on a regular basis will have a much greater chance of success if you start off with one major behavior change at a time. Create one success habit at a time. That's what all highly successful people do. Remember it is through persistent action that you will win.

WRITING EXERCISE

› Make a list in order of priority of what you will need to do persistently to achieve your goal.

› How often do I need to do that top action?

› After doing that action for a few days, how does it feel to do this thing?

› What do I do when I have the urge to slack off or quit?

› How would I describe the tool of persistence to someone who has not read this book?

Get ready! This powerful tool will absolutely draw your goals towards you

Visioneering comes from two words we all know. Vision and engineering. Vision is simply to see something, be it real or imagined. To engineer is to apply scientific principles to a problem. The term Visioneering was coined in the 40's and used by the Alcoa company as a tool for its executives to create massive success. It worked!

It's reported that Disney himself used Visioneering to change a swath of swampland in the middle of Florida into one of the world's most sought-after destinations, *Disneyworld*.

How it works: Visioneering is the practice of regularly writing and thinking about what it is you want to achieve. The habit of doing this will keep you strong and focused.

Pick a spot where you won't be disturbed and set a timer for ten to fifteen minutes each day to write about your dreams and goals. It doesn't matter if you have any idea how you will achieve them, just write.

You can think of this as a stream of consciousness process. Just write whatever comes to your mind.

Get a new journal and special pen if you can afford to do so. Make this a ceremonial pen. It's not necessary to go back and read your daily writing; the main thing is that you develop the habit of Visioneering daily.

Each day will be different. Some days you may write about what it will feel like once you have achieved your goals. Others you'll write about how your life will change once you've gotten there.

In addition to writing daily, I want you to think and daydream daily about the same goals. In the same way as writing, you'll devote a few minutes daily to thinking about your success. Imagine you have already achieved your goals, imagine how your life would change and how it will feel to have the success you have been dreaming about. This is important so don't neglect the mental aspect of Visioneering.

With Visioneering you always want to keep it positive and write as if it's happening or has already happened.

This tool of Visioneering crosses over all the sections of this book, that's how powerful it is. It's a powerful tool for maintaining a winning "CAN-DO" mindset. Visioneering is an essential habit to get into and doing it regularly will keep you inspired and give you needed support when times get tough and you want to quit.

This is a habit I want you to do daily. Don't beat yourself up if you miss a day but set the intention to do it daily as this will yield the greatest benefit. Get a fresh journal and pen and sit down and write for at least 10 minutes every day about what it is you want. Write anything that comes to mind as long as it's positive. Don't worry if you feel like your rambling; that's OK, no one will read this but you.

Write about you and your life once you have achieved your goals. See yourself in your mind's eye as that bestselling author, CEO of a successful company, Husband or Wife to the most wonderful partner, having the perfect body, or that deep spiritual connection you have always wanted. Whatever it is you're going to accomplish, vision about it daily.

In addition to writing, I want you to think (daydream) for at least 10 minutes daily about what it is you want to accomplish. Think as if it's already happened. Have fun with it.

WRITING EXERCISE

› Keep a Visioneering journal. Write daily for at least 10 minutes about what you're going to accomplish.

Don't judge or censor yourself—just write. Write about yourself and your life in the future as if you have already achieved your dream. There are so many aspects of you and your life once you have had your great success so enjoy writing about any and all of them.

› Daydream for at least 10 minutes daily about life once you have achieved your goal.

› How are you feeling about yourself after a week of Visioneering?

› How would you describe Visioneering Io someone who has not read this book?

TOOL # 21 — SELF-CARE: REST, FOOD, DRUGS/ALCOHOL, & EXERCISE

"TO KEEP THE BODY IN GOOD HEALTH
IS A DUTY...OTHERWISE WE SHALL
NOT BE ABLE TO KEEP OUR MIND
STRONG AND CLEAR." —BUDDHA

This tool will help you become aware of your self-care habits

I consider self-care as a tool for one huge reason. For you to make great changes and achieve big goals, you will need all your available mental and physical strength, clarity, and focus. Having a healthy and fit body and mind can be essential to having the energy to achieve your goals. Getting exercise, enough sleep, eating well, and limiting drugs and alcohol are three important habits to develop. They will give you that energy plus much more.

Admittedly self-care is a huge topic. However, for purposes of this book, I'm going to simply say that each one of you has the ability to figure out what's the right amount of physical exercise, sleep, an optimal diet, the right amount of alcohol or drug use if at all, for you. Everyone is different; for some a few drinks a week won't matter. Others will feel it necessary to abstain during periods of peak performance.

Same with diet, exercise, and sleep; you may find you need more or less of these during this highly creative and productive time. Honor your body and your ability to know yourself.

Remember, this is a time when you are trying to accomplish great things. It's different than life as usual. So treat this period differently. Just because you give up drinking or sugar or begin to exercise for 30 minutes a day while you're accomplishing your goals, it's not a life sentence. You may return to enjoying those things at a later time when your need for clarity, energy, and persistence are not as great.

Figure out what changes in your self-care routine are needed to feel strong and healthy and be at the top of your game.

PRACTICING SELF-CARE

This tool will help you develop awareness about your routines and that's the key most important first step in making changes. So no getting down on yourself if you see things you don't like and want to change. Instead, pat yourself on the back and congratulate yourself for your willingness to look at your behaviors. Anytime you have a negative thought about yourself use the reframe tool. Take a deep breath, ask yourself "so what do I want" and insert that new thought.

During the next week or however long you want, as you go through your life, notice your sleep, eating, resting, exercise, and partying behaviors. Without judgment or negative self-talk ask yourself, "Is this working to help me or hinder me in achieving my goals?" If you feel changes could be made to make you more powerful, ask yourself, "What could I do differently?" Begin to make those changes according to your new insights.

You may find you need more information on what's optimal for you in any category of self-care. Get that information. Use your ability to research and find what's right for you. Whatever additional support you need, get it. Make the decision to bring your behaviors in line with your goals and the magic will happen.

WRITING ASSIGNMENT

› What changes have you identified that will enhance your ability to achieve your goals?

› How are you feeling about this awareness?

› Will you use additional tools to make those changes and If so what are they?

› How would you explain the tool of self-care to someone who has not read this book?

FINAL THOUGHTS

Now that you have finished the book, consider going back to those tools that you feel will be most helpful in your pursuits. Practice them until you are completely comfortable and can feel their benefit. It's perfectly okay if you feel drawn to a single tool. Spend as much time with that tool as you feel is helpful. You will know when it's time to move on. Trust your instincts on this.

I, for instance, have made some of these tools daily habits; visioneering, reframing and segmenting are three tools that are completely integrated into my life. I use them daily and rely on them as I would electricity or water to keep me sane and moving forward toward my goals, while others I use occasionally, depending on what I'm doing. There is no right or wrong way to use this book, so make it yours.

Now go fearlessly toward your dreams. Don't quit if things get hard. Believe in yourself, find your source of inspiration, drink that in, and always support yourself!

I love this quote by Steve Jobs:

"TECHNOLOGY IS NOTHING. WHAT'S IMPORTANT IS THAT YOU **HAVE FAITH IN PEOPLE**, THAT THEY'RE BASICALLY SMART, AND IF YOU GIVE THEM THE TOOLS, THEY WILL DO WONDERFUL THINGS WITH THEM."

Writing Excercises in order of appearance:

TOOL #1   KNOWING YOUR "WHY"

WRITING EXCERCISE

› What is my "Y" statement?

› How does it feel being crystal clear about my why?

› Where can I put this statement where I will
see it often?

› How would I explain knowing your "Y" to someone
who has not read this book yet?

TOOL #2   GETTING CLEAR ON YOUR
VISION OR GOALS

WRITING EXERCISE

› Write out your vision of yourself. Go into as much
detail as possible.

› Why do I want this in my life?

› What goals will I need to accomplish to achieve
my vision?

› Prioritize your goals in order of importance to you.

- › How will my life change once I have achieved my goals/vision?

- › How do you feel having gotten in touch with your vision/goals?

- › Keep a daily record of what you have done to accomplish your goal no matter how big or small.

- › How would you explain the importance of goals setting to someone who has not read this book?

TOOL #3 THE FLASHLIGHT

WRITING EXERCISE

- › Write out your vision of yourself. Go into as much detail as possible.

- › Why do I want this in my life?

- › What goals will I need to accomplish to achieve my vision?

- › Prioritize your goals in order of importance to you.

- › How will my life change once I have achieved my goals/vision?

- › How do you feel having gotten in touch with your vision/goals?

- › Keep a daily record of what you have done to accomplish your goal no matter how big or small.

> How would you explain the importance of goals setting to someone who has not read this book?

TOOL #4 THE RESET BUTTON OR CANCEL CANCEL

WRITING EXERCISE

In your journal, answer these questions daily or weekly.

> How did it feel using this tool?

> What have I learned about myself from using this tool?

> Why is it important to reset my negative thoughts?

> How would I describe this tool to others who have not yet read this book?

TOOL #5 THE REFRAME.... SO WHAT DO I WANT INSTEAD OF WHAT I DON'T WANT?

WRITING EXCERCISE

> What is the change I want most in my life now?

> Why do I want this change to happen?

> How will I feel once I have accomplished this?

> What will my life change once this happens?

› How did it feel using this tool?

› How has using this tool changed me?

› How would I describe this tool to someone who has not read this book?

TOOL #6 UNDERSTANDING THE EFFECT NEGATIVE AND POSITIVE INFLUENCES, INCLUDING FAMILY AND FRIENDS, HAVE ON YOUR ABILITY TO MAKE POSITIVE CHANGES AND REACH YOUR GOALS

WRITING EXCERCISE

› Make a list of people who are positive influences for you during this period of change.

› Make a list of people who are negative influences for you during this period of change.

› Write a brief description of why limiting negative influences and surrounding yourself with posi-tive influences is important for your success during this period of change.

TOOL #7 AFFIRMATIONS: HOW TO USE THEM SO THEY REALLY WORK

› Make a list of your top 3 affirmations using the correct beginning.

› How is it feeling saying them?

› What's your believability factor when you say them?

› If one still feels a blt unbelievable, then change the beginning to make it more believable.

TOOL #8 SEGMENTING

WRITING EXCERCISE

› List 5 segments you identified today.

› For each segment write the ideal outcome you imagined.

› How close was the oulcome to the one you preprogrammed?

› How is it feeling using this tool?

› How would you describe Segmenting to someone who hasn't read this book?

TOOL #9 DON'T OVERTHINK IT, ESPECIALLY AT NIGHT

› Keep an overthinking log over the course of a week and jot down when you find yourself overthinking.

› After a day or two of this, jot down what method you use to stop the overthinking.

› In your overthinking log, note any progress you notice regarding overthinking.

› Briefly describe this tool of not overthinking to someone who has not read this book.

TOOL #10 FIND YOUR SOURCE(S) OF INSPIRATION

WRITING EXCERCISE

› What did it feel like asking for your sources of inspiration to be revealed to you?

› Where and when did you most feel a sense of inspiration?

› What did that inspiration feel like?

› What is your level of trust in your feelings of being inspired?

› After a few days do you notice a change in your

belief about being inspired?

> What is it you want most in your life right now?

> Why do you want this change to happen?

> How strong is your desire for this change to happen?

> How would you describe the tool of locating your source(s) of inspiration to another person?

TOOL #11 CREATE A POSITIVE SUPPORT SYSTEM DURING THIS PERIOD OF BIG CHANGE

WRITING EXERCISE

> Make a list of your support team.

> How did you feel when you realized you needed a support system?

> How did you feel asking for people to be on your support team?

> What were their reactions like when you asked them to be on your side?

> How would you explain this tool to someone who has not read this book?

> What is the difference between emotional and practical support?

TOOL #12 TIME MANAGEMENT & THE TIME LOG

› What did you learn about your use of time from keeping your log?

› How do you feel as you gain clarity over your use of time?

› What productive activities are you doing enough of?

› What unproductive activities are you doing too much of?

› How much time can you re-allocate for more productive activities?

› What activities would you like to do more of that will help you achieve your goal?

› How much time can you devote to those positive activities beginning now?

› How would you describe the Time Log to someone who has not read this book?

TOOL #13 THE WILL-DO LIST

WRITING EXCERCISE

> › Make your daily will-do list.

> › Cross off each action once you have completed it.

> › How did I feel today using this tool?

> › What kinds of things can I include or exclude from this list to better reach my goal?

> › How would I explain this tool to someone looking to reach a big goal?

TOOL #14 STAY CONNECTED TO YOUR SOURCE OF INSPIRATION AND USE THAT GUIDANCE OFTEN

WRITING EXCERCISE

> › What inspires me?

> › What inspiring activities am I doing regularly?

> › What inspiration did I receive from that activity?

> › How often am I doing them?

> › How does it feel incorporating inspirational activities into my daily routine?

- › What changes if any am I noticing as a result making inspirational activities a habit?

- › How would I describe this tool of staying connected to my source of inspiration to another person?

TOOL #15 REGULARLY USE YOUR SUPPORT SYSTEM, ESPECIALLY WHEN TIMES GET TOUGH

WRITING EXCERCISE

- › List those people who are your supports.

- › How does it feel having a support team?

- › Write about a time you used your support person.

- › What was the result of using that person for support, how did that change you?

- › Now that you have experience with a support network, do you feel you need to make any changes to your network? If so, what changes would you make?

- › How is your support network affecting your ability to reach your goal?

TOOL #16 HAVING AN ATTITUDE
OF GRATITUDE

› How did it feel thinking about 3 things you were grateful daily?

› What tools are you using to remind yourself to do this daily?

› How has becoming grateful changed the way you think and feel about yourself and your life?

› How would you describe this tool "Developing an Attitude of Gratitude" to others?

TOOL #17 GET COMFORTABLE WITH
BEING UNCOMFORTABLE

WRITING EXCERCISE

› What actions did I recently take towards my goal?

› How comfortable or uncomfortable was I before taking each action?

› How did I feel upon completing each action?

› What did I do or say to help me start those actions I was most uncomfortable with?

› Write a short statement on why it's important to become comfortable with being uncomfortable.

TOOL #18 DEVELOP A HABIT OF LIFELONG LEARNING

WRITING EXCERCISE

› What materials do I want to begin using for my regular learning?

› How often will I use them?

› After a few days, how am I feeling as a result of my ongoing learning?

› How would I describe this tool to someone who has not read this book?

TOOL #19 PERSISTENCE

WRITING EXERCISE

› Make a list in order of priority of what you will need to do persistently to achieve your goal.

› How often do I need to do that top action?

› After doing that action for a few days, how does it feel to do this thing?

› What do I do when I have the urge to slack off or quit?

› How would I describe the tool of persistence to someone who has not read this book?

TOOL #20 VISIONEERING

› Keep a Visioneering journal. Write daily for at least 10 minutes about what you're going to accomplish. Don't judge or censor yourself—just write. Write about yourself and your life in the future as if you have already achieved your dream. There are so many aspects of you and your life once you have had your great success so enjoy writing about any and all of them.

› Daydream for at least 10 minutes daily about life once you have achieved your goal.

› How are you feeling about yourself after a week of Visioneering?

› How would you describe Visioneering to someone who has not read this book?

TOOL #21 SELF-CARE: REST, FOOD, DRUGS/ALCOHOL & EXERCISE

WRITING EXCERCISE

› What changes have you identified that will enhance your ability to achieve your goals?

› How are you feeling about this awareness?

› Will you use additional tools to make those changes and If so what are they?

› How would you explain the tool of self-care to
someone who has not read this book?

To contact Evan Lacon,
you can email him at
Finishing21@gmail.com

Made in the USA
Columbia, SC
10 November 2017